Combatting Overthinking and Anxiety: Living a Happy and Purposeful Life

Julia L. Ferrati

Published by Julia L. Ferrati, 2024.

COMBATTING OVERTHINKING AND ANXIETY: LIVING A HAPPY AND PURPOSEFUL LIFE

First edition. August 21, 2024.

Copyright © 2024 Julia L. Ferrati.

ISBN: 979-8227688989

Written by Julia L. Ferrati.

Also by Julia L. Ferrati

Psicologia

Autostima: Scopri le Tecniche per Credere in te Stesso e Raggiungere i tuoi Obiettivi, Aumentare l'Intelligenza Emotiva e Rafforzare la Fiducia in te e Gestire le Emozioni per Migliorare la tua Vita

Crescita Personale: Scopri il Potere del Pensiero Positivo per Giungere alla Felicità, Credere in te Stesso e Raggiungere i tuoi Obiettivi Personali. La Guida Motivazionale per Arrivare al Successo.

PNL: Scopri la Psicologia Oscura Attraverso le Tecniche Proibite della Manipolazione e Persuasione Mentale, Interpreta il Linguaggio non Verbale Grazie alla Programmazione Neuro Linguistica

Linguaggio del Corpo: Come Analizzare e Interpretare il Linguaggio non Verbale Attraverso gli Atteggiamenti Inconsci, Scopri Come Leggere la Mente e Sviluppare al Meglio la tua Intelligenza Emotiva

Standalone

Combatting Overthinking and Anxiety: Living a Happy and Purposeful Life

Table of Contents

INTRODUCTION 1

CHAPTER 1 3

THE IMPACT OF OVERTHINKING ON DAILY LIFE ... 5

CHAPTER 2 9

LINK BETWEEN OVERTHINKING AND ANXIETY AND THE SCIENCE BEHIND BOTH 11

CHAPTER 3 21

IDENTIFY YOUR PATTERNS 23

CHAPTER 4 29

BREAK THE CYCLE 31

CHAPTER 5 49

A PERSONALIZED ANTI-ANXIETY PLAN 51

CONCLUSION 61

About the Author: Julia L. Ferrati 63

COMBATTING OVERTHINKING AND ANXIETY

Living a Happy and Purposeful Life

Julia L. Ferrati

INTRODUCTION

I wrote this book with one goal in mind. To be your partner on the road to a quieter, more focused mind.

Whether you have suffered from overthinking and anxiety for years or you are just beginning to sense their effects, the words in front of you were not written merely to offer temporary relief but to arm you with the tools that can help you break the cycle forever. You will become the master of a healthy relationship with your thoughts, in which you will not constantly be at their mercy.

By the end, you'll have sure strategies that you can use to face life's challenges with greater ease and confidence.

I hope you reap the fruit of this knowledge so abundantly that you are able to sow the seed too.

CHAPTER 1

3

THE IMPACT OF OVERTHINKING ON DAILY LIFE

Overthinking is a feeling most of us have experienced at one time or another. It's a lousy feeling when the mind doesn't seem to rest.

For many, overthinking isn't an occasional nuisance—it's an ever-present demon. And it might seem harmless at first; after all, isn't it better to think things through thoroughly?

As a habit, overthinking can sometimes become a mumbo jumbo of excessive thoughts that rob you of your peace.

The connection between your mind and body is powerful, and if you are caught in a cycle of overthinking, it will lead to physical issues such as headaches and fatigue.

One of the most common physical effects of overthinking is insomnia. When your mind is full of worry and racing thoughts, it's difficult to relax enough to fall asleep. Instead of floating away into a restful sleep, you may find yourself lying awake, replaying events from the day or worrying about the future. This restless state can keep you up for hours, and even when you do manage to sleep, it's often not restful.

This lack of quality sleep depletes you and leaves you feeling exhausted and sluggish the next day, creating a vicious cycle in which you are bound to overthink simply because you were already way too tired. It affects your body so negatively due to the stress response that this creates when you overthink.

In a vicious circle of worry and anxiety over whatever is ailing you, your body reacts as if it is a real danger. This signals the body to release cortisol and adrenaline. They prepare your body to deal for danger, making your heart race, muscles tense, and senses alert. Very useful in short bursts, but when activated over and over through overthinking, it can be responsible for a host of long-term health issues, such as high blood pressure, digestive issues, and heart disease.

Overthinking doesn't only affect you, but also the people around you. It can weigh your relationships down when you keep overthinking, replay conversations, or worry about what others might think. In personal relations, it would create unnecessary tension if you are questioning all the time whether what you said is right and worrying that your partner is upset with you. Instead of enjoying time together, you might find yourself fixated on small details, interpreting innocent actions or words as signs of deeper problems.

Moreover, when you're consumed by your thoughts, you might seem distracted, distant, or even disinterested even with the presence of your loved one which can be hurtful to them. As a result of this emotional distance, both of you can start feeling distant from each other and lonely. It erodes with time the very important base on which trust and intimacy are built in any relationship.

It is no different in professional relationships. Overanalyzing things within a second can delay decisions, which may turn away good opportunities. Being afraid to express views or feeling embarrassed about your opinion not being good enough might make your peers and even superiors not trust you much because they would perceive you as indecisive and not confident. It could be a detractor from growth in your career because opportunities such as promotion may pass you by.

Overthinking also creates misconceptions at the workplace: when you are too much worried about what other people think of you, it may be easy to misconstrue their actions or words and see criticism where there is none, potentially leading to conflict or tension that is otherwise unwarranted with colleagues when you react defensively or withdraw from collaboration. This can cause some great harm when in a team as it disrupts communication flow and productivity.

Most people who overthink end up being big-time procrastinators. Productivity is all art of getting things done efficiently and effectively. But when you overthink, your mind finds itself stuck in a cycle of 'what ifs' and 'maybes,' causing you to procrastinate as you put off taking action out of fear that you'll make the wrong choice. This then leads tasks that should be simple and straightforward to take much longer to complete, reducing overall productivity.

Lack of focus is also another thing caused by overthinking. When your mind is filled with racing thoughts, it's hard to concentrate on the task at hand. You might find yourself starting on one task, only to get distracted by worries about another, and then another. This constant switching between thoughts can make it difficult to maintain the deep focus needed to complete tasks efficiently.

Overthinking can also lead to "analysis paralysis," where you're so focused on analyzing every possible outcome that you're unable to make a decision or move forward with an idea. This can be especially detrimental in creative work, where innovation often comes from taking bold, uncertain steps into the unknown.

CHAPTER 2

LINK BETWEEN OVERTHINKING AND ANXIETY AND THE SCIENCE BEHIND BOTH

The Link

Analyzing, ruminating, or obsessing over things that don't necessarily need that much attention, is pretty much what overthinking is.

Anxiety, on the other hand, is the emotion we've all felt at some point—before a big exam, during a job interview, or when facing an uncertain future. But for some people, anxiety isn't just a temporary feeling. It can become a constant presence that makes daily life feel overwhelming.

Sometimes, anxiety has accompanying side effects, such as muscle tension, and may cause stomach aches or even nausea. It causes dizziness or a feeling of light-headedness in some people. Long-term anxiety weakens the immune system, thereby causing it to be susceptible to various diseases. It is also physically very tiring; sometimes it wears you out such that even if you haven't done anything physically strenuous, you feel utterly wiped out.

Anxiety affects your thoughts and feelings psychologically. People with anxiety frequently experience persistent thoughts about something unpleasant that is going to happen. You will find yourself having a repetitive worry loop about things that are out of your control or that haven't even happened yet.

Anxiety may also lead to avoidance behavior toward situations or places that trigger fear or worry. Over time, this avoidance can limit your life and keep you from things that you might enjoy or need to do, like going to work or hanging out with your friends. It can lead to loneliness and depression, fueling one mental health problem with the other.

Overthinking and anxiety are just two sides of one coin. For example, you could find yourself sometimes stuck in a chain of thoughts with no end, worrying about the what-ifs. The most probable is that you will overthink it and get anxious in such a loop. Thereby, it is easy to see how overthinking may be fueling anxiety and vice versa—when the mind continuously produces negative scenarios, it becomes almost impossible not to get anxious. And when you are anxious, the looping thoughts just seem to lead to even more overthinking. The more anxious you feel, the more you're likely to overthink so that you can gain some sense of control over your worries. But instead of finding solutions, you often end up creating more problems in your mind.

One way these two feed off each other is through the "what if" trap. When anxious, people focus on the worst-case scenarios. You might find yourself thinking, "What if I flunk this test?" or "What if something happens at work?" Overthinking then takes those worries and runs with them, making you analyze every possible bad outcome.

Overthinking can lead to an increased sense of self-doubt. When one is in a constant state of second-guessing themselves, it makes it quite easy to start doubting one's own abilities. This lack of confidence fuels anxiety into making one worry about how they are not good enough or how they will never measure up to something. The more you feel that, the more anxious you feel, and the more you overthink

The Science

It is kind of amazing to think that our brain works all the time processing everything we see, hear, and feel without our knowledge. At times, how the brain processes thought and emotion feels mysterious, but we can get a basic grasp of these cognitive processes to make sense of our thinking and feeling.

Cognition involves how our brain interprets information. Picture your brain like a supercomputer, constantly bombarded with input: sounds, sights, smells, touches—all going into the mix, out of which come thoughts and emotions. The process takes place so quickly and effortlessly that most of the time, we are not even aware of it. Still, it is pretty far in the background, yet of great consequence to our experiences.

One of the key parts of cognitive processing is perception. Perception is the process of interpreting information brought in through our senses. For instance, you see a red apple; your eyes send the information to the brain about the color, shape, and size of the apple. The brain then processes this information and tells you that what you are looking at is an apple.

Once the brain has processed this sensory information, it moves on to thoughts. A thought is actually the interpretation and meaning that the brain thought it saw or heard. It could be anything from choosing that the apple is delicious to remembering your allergy to apples. Thoughts are continuously constructed by the brain from all the processed information and reflected in how you feel and what you do next.

Emotions come with thoughts. In fact, it is often thoughts that stimulate the onset of emotions. For example, if you think about something that makes you happy, your brain automatically produces feelings of joy, right? On the contrary, if you think about something that worries you, your brain might trigger feelings of anxiety. But it's not just about the thoughts and emotions themselves—how we interpret them also matters. This is where cognitive processes like reasoning and judgment come into play.

Reasoning helps us make sense of our thoughts and emotions, while judgment helps us decide how to react to them. For example, if one is feeling anxious, the brain will use reasoning in order to figure out why they are anxious, and judgment to decide whether that anxiety is something they need to act on or not.

Then there's that little part of the brain, which acts as an alarm system on constant alert for possible danger. This small region of the brain is known as the amygdala, which is considered to be the fear center of the brain. If your brain senses anything dangerous—like a loud noise or an intimidating situation—an amygdala reaction is triggered.

The amygdala transmits signals to the rest of your brain and body in mobilizing it for a fight or to flee from the danger. While great at keeping you safe, the amygdala can also be the very cause of anxiety when there is actually no real danger. Your heart starts pounding so that more blood can go to your muscles, your breathing begins to speed up to take in more air, and your senses sharpen so that you remain alert for no good reason.

The amygdala doesn't always get it right. This can happen in everyday situations when you're just thinking about something that worries you.

The amygdala is also involved in memory consolidation, especially for fear-related memories. This means that if you have had some scary or traumatic experience in the past, your amygdala may overreact in the future when encountering similar stimuli, even when there is no actual danger. For example, an amygdala would cause anxiety when one goes into a car after one has been involved in an accident, although there is actually no danger. Understanding the role of the amygdala is helpful in understanding why anxiety can sometimes feel so overwhelming; it's like your brain's alarm system is going off too often, signaling danger when there isn't any.

And then, there's the prefrontal cortex is the part of the brain where most of the superior functions that qualify us as human beings are based, such as decision-making, planning, and reasoning. But just as much as the prefrontal cortex can be such a handy part of the brain for problem-solving and thinking into the future, it can also be responsible for overthinking. Knowing how that part of your brain works can help you understand why it sometimes gets stuck in overdrive, which is when the frustrating cycle of one thought after another takes over.

The prefrontal cortex rests right in front, behind the forehead. It is often called the "executive center" of the brain due to its role in helping a person make decisions, plan for the future, and control impulses. The prefrontal cortex is the part of the brain that basically does most of the heavy lifting when you're trying to solve a problem, be it what's for dinner or how to deal with a difficult situation at work. It contemplates alternatives, deliberates over options, and selects the optimal course of action.

However, this ability to future think and contemplate different outcomes is also the very reason for the prefrontal cortex being so prone to overthink. Instead of making a decision and moving on, the prefrontal cortex becomes ensnared in a loop of second-guessing the situation and being worried about all that might be done wrong. This happens especially when you're dealing with uncertainty or stress. Your prefrontal cortex may begin working doubly hard if the stakes are high, trying to calculate every which way in order not to make a mistake.

Overthinking is when the prefrontal cortex just can't seem to know when to stop. It seems it is never going to come to any conclusion and is just going to keep throwing up more questions, doubts, and what-ifs instead of reaching a conclusion. One might find oneself going over the same thoughts in different ways again and again without reaching a solution.

Another way in which the prefrontal cortex contributes to overthinking is self-reflection. This part of your brain thinks about your own thoughts and actions, and it's important for learning from past experiences and ways to make yourself better. But if self-reflection turns to self-criticism, it very often will start a cycle of overthinking. You might begin questioning every little thing that you do, play back past mistakes in your head, or be overly concerned about what others think. That is the type of overthinking that might really hurt your self-esteem and make you feel trapped in your own head.

The prefrontal cortex plays a big role in good management of emotions. It helps you drive your feelings and respond to anything thoughtfully. But when emotions get more pronounced, then the prefrontal cortex can become overwhelmed, and it becomes harder to think through the matter. This is probably when overthinking tends to occur, as your brain tries to make sense of the emotions you're going through and work out how to react to them. You find yourself analyzing feelings over and over again, trying to understand why you feel a certain way and what to do about it."

And finally, there's the neurotransmitters which are tiny chemical messengers that play a vital role in how our brain functions by transmitting signals between nerve cells, or neurons. These chemicals, including serotonin, dopamine, and cortisol, are responsible for regulating everything from your mood to your stress levels.

When a neuron needs to communicate with another neuron, it releases a neurotransmitter into the gap between them, known as a synapse. The neurotransmitter then binds to receptors on the neighboring neuron, passing along the message. This rapid process allows your brain to communicate with your body, controlling everything from movements to emotions.

Serotonin is one of the most well-known neurotransmitters, often referred to as the "feel-good" chemical. It plays a crucial role in regulating mood, sleep, and appetite. When serotonin levels are sufficient, you're likely to feel calm, happy, and content. However, low serotonin levels can lead to feelings of sadness, irritability, or anxiety, which is why serotonin is often linked to depression. Many antidepressant medications work by increasing serotonin levels in the brain.

Dopamine, another key neurotransmitter, is sometimes called the "reward" chemical. It's involved in how we experience pleasure and motivation. When you do something enjoyable—like eating your favorite food, achieving a goal, or spending time with loved ones—your brain releases dopamine, creating a sense of satisfaction and encouraging you to repeat the behavior.

However, excessive dopamine can lead to addictive behaviors, as the brain craves more of the reward. Conversely, low dopamine levels are associated with conditions such as Parkinson's disease and can also contribute to feelings of low energy and lack of motivation.

Cortisol, often known as the stress hormone, is another crucial neurotransmitter that your body releases in response to stress. When stress becomes chronic, it can lead to consistently high levels of cortisol, which may negatively impact your health. Elevated cortisol levels can interfere with sleep, weaken your immune system, and increase the risk of anxiety and depression.

Serotonin, dopamine, and cortisol are just a few examples of the many neurotransmitters that shape how you think, feel, and behave. These chemicals work together in a delicate balance to ensure your brain functions properly. However, when this balance is disrupted, it can result in various mental health challenges, including anxiety, depression, addiction, and stress-related disorders.

Now that we have learned the link between overthinking and anxiety and the science behind both, it is time to move on to recognizing your personal triggers and the types of these disorders that you might be dealing with. This, we shall thoroughly discuss in the next chapter.

CHAPTER 3

IDENTIFY YOUR PATTERNS

History is full of such famous overthinkers. All these people prove that even the greatest, most significant contributors to human civilization were not immune to the pitfalls of overthinking.

Charles Darwin

Charles Darwin, the naturalist responsible for On the Origin of Species, had a reputation for overthinking.

For years, Darwin hesitated in publishing his theories of natural selection because of the massive backlash and possible criticism that would be pointed at him from not just the scientific but the public community as well. This delayed the publication of his very enlightening book by more than two decades.

Ludwig van Beethoven

Ludwig van Beethoven. Beethoven was an absolute perfectionist; he would always work around revising his compositions in pursuit of pure musical perfection. His letters show a man at the mercy of doubts and anxiety.

These historical examples prove that overthinking is not peculiar to modern times; rather, it is what has plagued some of the most brilliant minds in history. The important thing is to fight it so that it does not hamper your speed in life.

Now, if these people in history had allowed overthinking and anxiety to paralyze them, they never would have done what they did.

In combatting overthinking and anxiety, you need to identify your patterns which are your triggers, and the types you're experiencing.

Identify your triggers

It seems at times that overthinking and anxiety just swear out of thin air and start making themselves most comfortable in the mind when you least expect them to visit. The thing is, they are mostly triggered by certain situations, thoughts, or experiences.

It's almost like finding a key to a locked door. The realization of what exactly makes your mind start racing or your heart pound is the thing that is going to give you the keys to dealing better with it. To know common triggers of both overthinking and anxiety can take you back in control and stop those feelings from ruling your life.

Uncertainty, probably, is the most common trigger of overthinking and anxiety. When you don't have clarity regarding what's going to transpire next in your life, it's absolutely spontaneous that your mind will start filling those gaps. But more often than not, it will do so with worst-case scenarios. Be it waiting for the results of medical tests or a job interview, or even how someone feels about you, the possibilities are really endless.

Another major trigger is the fear of failure. That will make you question every single decision that you make—yes, not only the big ones in life but even daily ones, like sending an email or calling somebody.

Past experiences can be such a very strong trigger, too. If you have passed through an exceptionally tough or traumatic experience, then some situations and memories can easily take you back to that feeling. For example, if you have had bad past experiences in connection with public speaking, then just the mere thought of having to present will very likely send your mind racing with thoughts, tangling them up in anxiety.

Another very common trigger, however, is social situations. The fear of judgment, the need to fit in, creates a lot of overthinking. You may feel concerned about what others think of you, if you said the right thing, or if you left a good impression. This kind of thinking is tiring and can turn simple interactions into sources of stress.

It's not only large social gatherings; even just a conversation one-on-one can trigger overthinking if you're worried about how you're being perceived.

But another surprising trigger of overthinking and anxiety can be your physical health. If you are not well because of lack of sleep, poor diet, or chronic illness, your head becomes more prone to shadier thoughts. Discomfort of the body easily flows into mental discomfort, more spanning you to move alongside patterns of overthinking. This is the reason it becomes very important how you take care of your body and your mind. By recognizing these common triggers, you shall be able to realize how you can manage overthinking and anxiety. Don't you think that if you know what has set off these kinds of emotions, then you can start to address them head-on?.

Identify your type(s)

Easy—it's only three kinds of overthinking: ruminating, worrying, perfectionism.

Ruminating means, to a large degree, replaying events from the past in your mind over and over again. Specifically, this could be concentrated on whatever went wrong or anything that you wish you could have changed. It is like running the replays of the same scene from a movie over and over again, but instead of enjoying it, you are stuck on those portions that make you feel bad. You catch yourself on some embarrassing thing you said, some mistake you made, or some conversation didn't turn out in your favor. Ruminating may create feelings of regret, shyness, and depression because you are stuck in the past without being able to turn around.

Worrying is directed at the future. Despite the fact that some things have not yet happened, and also perhaps might never really happen, worrying makes such entities feel very real in the present moment. It's like your brain is trying to predict the future, but instead it comes up with worst-case scenarios. You can be haunted by fears of failing an exam, losing a job, or getting sick. This makes you unable to enjoy the present because you're so preoccupied with what may go wrong in the future.

Perfectionism means that you have very high standards for yourself and become pretty obsessed with doing everything perfectly. Though this consideration can lend itself toward excellence, perfectionism can cause overthinking in which nothing feels good enough. You will rake through every last detail of a project for hours on end, fearing that things may not be just perfect or that you might botch it. This can make even simple tasks overwhelming because you are constantly doubting yourself, wondering if you will measure up. Perfectionism also hinders acting because of fear—producing mistakes is so significant that it eventually leads to doing nothing at all.

The good news is that once you realize the triggers and kinds that form the patterns keeping you in entrapment, you can begin to challenge them. For example, when you realize that you are ruminating over something, tell yourself that it is of the past and there is nothing you can change about it. When you feel a tendency to worry about the future, turn your attention to what you can control in the present. If perfectionism holds you back, remember that everybody makes mistakes and nobody is perfect.

CHAPTER 4

29

BREAK THE CYCLE

Breaking the cycle of overthinking and anxiety requires getting yourself into activities that will make you face-to-face with these disorders. You are more powerful and will always be, but it won't look like it until you put your power into action. Here are ways to do this:

- **Practice mindfulness to stay present.**

Attention in the present moment and without judgment basically characterizes mindfulness. You are not supposed to get your mind trapped in thoughts or allowed to wander on something else as you take note of what is happening at that very moment—be it through the sensation of your breath, the sounds around, or the taste of food.

While most people think of mindfulness as 'stopping thoughts,' it is more about the shift in one's relationship with them. One begins to develop how to observe thoughts and not be swept away by them through regular practice.

Start with Your Breath: The easiest form of mindfulness practice is breathing, so start there. Take a few minutes each day to sit in silence and just observe your process of breathing. Observe the sensation of air moving in and out of your body. If your mind strays, gently bring it back to your breath.

Mindful Eating: Another excellent way to bring about mindfulness into everyday life is through eating. Eat more slowly, without rushing your meals or getting diverted by other activities while eating. Savor each and every bite, noting the taste, texture, smell, and all else associated with eating. This enhances your eating pleasure and keeps you oriented and clear of overthinking during mealtimes.

Body Scan Meditation: The body scan is just bringing mindfulness to different parts of the human body at a time, where you start from the toes upwards to the head, noticing whatever sensation may happen to exist within you. This type of exercise helps a person stay connected with his body as it associative releases tension and might become very useful in stressful or anxious moments.

Mindful walking: This is a rather simple way to carry out mindfulness on the move. While walking, feel the touch of your feet on the ground and the rhythm of steps—don't take your phone along, just be there in that walk.

This means mindfulness in activities like daily tasks. You need not take extra time to meditate, you can practice mindfulness during your daily routines. While washing dishes, folding clothes, or even when you are brushing your teeth, focus on what is happening. Observe the body actions, feelings and surroundings to avoid wandering of your mind.

- **Use Cognitive Behavioral Therapy**

CBT is a very efficient way to deal with negative thoughts. The kind of treatment is premised on the fact that all of your thoughts, emotions, and actions are interrelated. The gist of this principle is that negative thoughts create negative feelings and behaviors, which in turn help promote those negative thoughts.

In its course of action, CBT teaches the patient how to identify and challenge negative thinking and exchange such patterns with more positive and real ones.

First, Identify Negative Thoughts: Most of these are usually automatic thoughts, which simply crop up in your head without you knowing it. For instance, you may be thinking, "I'm going to fail," right before a huge presentation. The thing is to become sensitively aware of these thoughts when they occur.

Challenge the Negative Thoughts: Once you've identified a negative thought, the next step is to challenge it. Ask yourself questions like:

Is this thought based on facts or assumptions?

Have I been in a similar situation before, and how did it turn out?

What's the worst that could happen, and how would I deal with it?

What would I say to a friend who had this thought?

By questioning the validity of your negative thoughts, you can start to see them for what they are—just thoughts, not facts. This helps to reduce their power over you.

Reframe Negative Thoughts: Once you have challenged your negative thoughts, try to reframe them into something more positive or realistic. For example, instead of thinking, "I'm going to fail," reframe it to say, "I have prepared well, and I'll do my best." You are trying to make a balanced perspective; this does not require that you are overly optimistic about the future.

Use Thought Stopping: Thought stopping is a cognitive-behavioral technique in which a person interrupts the beginning of a negative thought. If you hear yourself thinking something negative, just say to yourself, "Stop," in your head or out loud. This simple act helps stop that negative spiral and brings your focus to other positive things.

Use positive affirmations: You can do this by replacing those negative thoughts with affirmations—thoughts that reflect a more balanced and positive view of who you are. For example, instead of thinking, "I'm not good enough," you could think, "But I'm capable and have strengths that I bring to the table." Saying such sentences over and over can make these positive thinking patterns quite strong.

Thought Diaries: Keep a diary of your thoughts, recording negative thoughts, the situations that provoked them, what you felt, and how you responded. It is this exercise that will enable both the following of progress over time and the identification of patterns of thought. It helps you think about possible ways you may reframe in similar situations.

Visualize the Outcome: Do not spend your time thinking about all worst-case scenarios. Use visualization to picture your success in the specific situation you worry about. Doing so will not only reduce anxiety but also help build your confidence.

- **Set boundaries by saying NO and prioritizing mental well-being.**

Boundaries are the invisible lines that delineate what you are willing to receive from others and from yourself. It protects your time, energy, and emotional space. Not having these boundaries makes one vulnerable to being overwhelmed, overcommitted, and stressed by trying to say "yes" to all things and people, mostly at the cost of oneself.

You set the limits for others in treating you, and you are showing that your well-being is important by setting boundaries. It does not mean you have to be harsh or unkind in this regard; rather, it means only being clear about your limits and sticking to them.

Know Your Limits: Setting limits begins with knowing your own limits. Take time to reflect on what is really within your capacity in terms of workload, social commitments, or requests for favors. This aids in maintaining a sense of when you really need to say no.

Start Small: If you find setting boundaries too overwhelming, start with the small things. For example, if you are one of those kinds who always says "yes" to every extra work asked from you, just refuse one small request. Do this and more to help build your confidence in setting limits, which makes bigger challenges easier to face later on.

Practice the Art of Saying No: Saying "no" is difficult, especially when you are not used to saying the word. Start with small exercises in how to say no firmly but respectfully. You don't have to linger on a long-winded explanation—sometimes just, "I can't take that on right now," is enough. Remember, it is okay to say "no" when in fact this will preserver your own well-being.

Clear Communication: Setting boundaries requires one to be clear with communication. State what you are and you are not comfortable with. For example, if you have to leave work at a particular time to avoid burnout, communicate that to your boss or colleagues. When a friend continues calling you very late at night, he or she could be violated by simply letting them know that you need to sleep but you can talk earlier.

Be Consistent: As soon as you have established a limit, remember to maintain it. If you give up and then say "yes" when you just said "no," this will only serve to disorient the other people and make it harder for them to respect your boundaries the next time. It helps to build your boundaries by showing that you literally mean what you say.

Don't Feel Guilty: So many of us feel guilty when we set boundaries, and it's important to remember that it's not at all selfish to take care of yourself. You can't pour from an empty cup, so with those limits in place, you'll reserve energy and mental space for times when you really need to be present.

Take Care of Your Mind: Ultimately, it all centers on your mental health. Setting boundaries is an integral part of your mental health. It could be taking time out for yourselves, saying 'no' to extra commitments, or just letting go of relationships that drain you off—whatever it is, it is imperative to take care of your well-being if you want to move towards a more balanced and whole life.

- **Grounding Techniques (Immediate actions to take when you find yourself overthinking)**

Grounding techniques are there to save the day by washing you out of the overthinking cycle and bringing your focus to the present moment. Such techniques are pretty simple, individual works that one can do at any place, at any time to help pacify the mind and cut down on stress. Let's look through some practical grounding techniques that help when overthinking.

    i. The 5-4-3-2-1 Technique

The 5-4-3-2-1 method is a simple way to connect with your surroundings using your five senses, which helps shift your focus away from your thoughts. Here's how it works:

5: Look around and name five things you can see. It could be anything—a book on the table, a picture on the wall, or the trees outside.

4: Identify four things you can touch. Feel the texture of your clothing, the cool surface of your desk, or the warmth of a cup in your hands.

3: Listen for three things you can hear. Maybe it's the sound of the wind, the hum of your computer, or distant voices.

2: Notice two things you can smell. This could be the scent of your coffee or the fresh air coming through the window.

1: Focus on one thing you can taste. It might be the lingering taste of your lunch or simply the freshness of your breath.

This technique helps you ground yourself in the present moment, making it easier to let go of overthinking.

    i. Deep Breathing

Deep breathing is a quick and effective way to calm your mind and body. Try this simple breathing exercise:

Inhale deeply through your nose for a count of four.

Hold your breath for a count of four.

Exhale slowly through your mouth for a count of four.

Repeat this cycle several times until you feel more relaxed.

Focusing on your breath helps interrupt the cycle of overthinking and brings your attention back to the present.

Physical Grounding

Engaging your body is another powerful way to stop overthinking. Here are a few physical grounding techniques you can try:

Stretch: Stand up and stretch your arms, legs, and back. Focus on the sensations in your muscles as you stretch.

Walk: Take a short walk, even if it's just around the room. Pay attention to how your feet feel as they touch the ground.

Hold an Object: Grab an object, like a stress ball or a smooth stone, and focus on how it feels in your hand. Notice its texture, weight, and temperature.

These physical activities help draw your mind away from overthinking and anchor you in the present.

● **Exercise**

Exercise releases certain chemicals into the system called endorphins. These are often referred to as the body's "feel-good" hormones because they can elevate your mood and put you in a state of well-being. Endorphins help alleviate stress and anxiety by pushing a pleasurable feeling through the body, something like that of morphine, only naturally and without the side effects.

If you don't exercise regularly, do small amounts with steps you can handle. You do not have to run a marathon in order to gain the advantages from exercise. Begin with a 10-minute walk around your neighborhood or a few minutes of stretching. What's important here is being consistent—aim to make physical activity a regular part of the day.

Do things that are fun. Exercise does not have to be a chore in your mind. If you enjoy dancing, swimming, hiking, or riding a bike, then get active with something you have a passion for. When you enjoy the activity you are doing, it is more likely you will continue to do it and develop a habit of physical activity.

Be on the lookout for opportunities throughout your day to be active. Take the steps instead of riding an elevator, walk or bike to work if practical, or do stretches during breaks. Even small bursts of activity can add up and be helpful in instances of anxiety.

Exercise with others: If you are someone who doesn't find it that motivating to exercise solo, take a group exercise class or get an exercise buddy. Exercising with others enables one to enjoy the experience more and gets extra social support, which is good for mental health, too.

Finally, set realizable target for yourself. This will keep you motivated and create a record of your progress. Just start small. For example, exercising three times per week should be possible, then graduate to a longer and more intense session as one is on an upward trajectory in fitness level.

- **Nutrition and Diet (Foods that can help manage anxiety and boost mental health)**

What you eat can greatly affect your overall feelings. Just as there are certain foods that could fuel your body, certain foods may help in keeping your mind or would be very great for a healthier mind. Fueling the right way will keep that anxious feeling at bay and boost your mental health. There are some foods to include in your diet for better mental wellbeing:

 i. Omega-3 Fatty Acids

Omega-3 fatty acids are essential fats that play a crucial role in brain health. They are found in high concentrations in the brain and are vital for cognitive function and emotional regulation. Foods rich in omega-3s include fatty fish like salmon, mackerel, and sardines. If you're not a fan of fish, you can also get omega-3s from flaxseeds, chia seeds, and walnuts. Studies have shown that omega-3s can help reduce symptoms of anxiety and depression by supporting the brain's neurotransmitter function.

 i. Complex Carbohydrates

Complex carbohydrates, like those found in whole grains, oats, quinoa, and brown rice, help stabilize blood sugar levels, which is important for keeping your mood balanced. These foods promote the production of serotonin, a neurotransmitter that has a calming effect on the brain. When your blood sugar is stable, you're less likely to experience mood swings or anxiety spikes.

i. Leafy Greens

Leafy greens like spinach, kale, and broccoli are packed with vitamins, minerals, and antioxidants that support brain health. They are particularly rich in folate (vitamin B9), which has been linked to reduced symptoms of depression and anxiety. Folate helps regulate mood by contributing to the production of serotonin and dopamine, two key neurotransmitters.

i. Fermented Foods

Your gut health is closely linked to your mental health, and eating fermented foods can help maintain a healthy gut microbiome. Foods like yogurt, kefir, sauerkraut, and kimchi contain probiotics—beneficial bacteria that support gut health. A healthy gut can lead to improved mental health by reducing inflammation and promoting the production of mood-regulating chemicals.

i. Berries

Berries such as blueberries, strawberries, and raspberries are high in antioxidants, which help protect your brain from oxidative stress. They also contain vitamin C, which can help lower levels of the stress hormone cortisol. Including a variety of berries in your diet can help protect your brain and reduce feelings of anxiety.

i.   Nuts and Seeds

Nuts and seeds, such as almonds, pumpkin seeds, and sunflower seeds, are excellent sources of magnesium, which plays a key role in regulating mood and stress levels. Magnesium helps relax muscles and nerves, making it an important mineral for reducing anxiety. Snack on a handful of nuts or sprinkle seeds on your meals to boost your intake.

i.   Dark Chocolate

Good news for chocolate lovers: dark chocolate (with at least 70% cocoa content) can help reduce anxiety. Dark chocolate contains flavonoids, which are antioxidants that improve blood flow to the brain and enhance cognitive function. It also contains magnesium and stimulates the production of endorphins, which can boost your mood. Enjoy dark chocolate in moderation as a treat that also supports your mental health.

- **Sleep Hygiene**

Sleep hygiene will help you get a better night of sleep. But on the flip side, if you want to experience optimal mental clarity and an improved mood, getting that good night's sleep is critical. Unfortunately, not everyone gets a good night's sleep! You can take a look at this article if you want tips on improving your sleep hygiene.

Implement Proper Sleep Timing

Going to bed and getting up at the same time every day, even on weekends, is one of the most important steps you can take in improving your sleep hygiene. Having our meals at the same time every day helps in regulating your body clock and sleep symptoms, making it easier for us to fall asleep early. You will eventually adapt to that running cycle and sleep better before/after your runs.

Establish a Soothing Sleep Routine

Creating a relaxing pre-sleep routine can let your body know it is time to start winding down. Read a book, take a warm bath, or soak in Epsom salt (one of my personal favorites) and do them 30-60 minutes before bedtime. Avoid stimulating activities such as dinner, watching TV, or using your phone and computer before bed because blue light from screens can affect the production of melatonin (sleep hormone), which will cause you to struggle to fall asleep.

Turn Your Bedroom Into a Conducive Sleep-Friendly Environment

Your bedroom should be a sleep oasis. The ideal sleeping environment is cool, dark, and quiet. Prepare blackout curtains to keep light out and earplugs or even a sound machine for white noise. Ensure your mattress and pillows are comfy. Note: If you are not satisfied with your bed, invest in good bedding options to sleep better.

Limit Naps

While napping can be a good way to make up for lost sleep due to sleeping less or poorly the night before, long naps during the day or one nap in particular that is different from what you did yesterday will disrupt your nighttime rest. If you must nap, limit it to 20-30 minutes and avoid napping in the late afternoon or evening.

• Create a Supportive Environment

The kinds of energy, especially in anxiety management, we keep around can affect how you feel greatly. Nurturing the right environment induces a state of grace where you are calmer, more focused, and able to cope with stress. Switch up your room to create a more calming surrounding that enhances mental health.

Declutter Your Space

Clutter can be distressing, and it directly impacts stress levels. It is difficult to focus, let alone relax, when your environment is unorganized. We can begin by decluttering our space, whether it is home, your workspace, or even your car. Spend some time sifting through your things, dusting out the corners, and clearing away what is no longer needed to help you create that feeling of order. Being in a clean environment can keep the mind clear and energized, giving off more peace.

Incorporate Calming Colors

Our color choices stimulate emotional responses. Colors such as gentle blues, greens, and neutrals are calming colors that can help lessen all kinds of anxiety. Consider incorporating these shades into your surroundings, whether through wall paint, furniture items, or decorative pieces. Even small touches, like a blue pillow on the couch or a green plant in the corner, can influence your feelings about your space.

Use Natural Light

We all need natural light for our mental health. This can help with maintaining a healthy circadian rhythm, which will improve mood, energy levels, and deep sleep. Organize your home or workspace to receive as much daylight as possible. Pull back your curtains to let natural light in and take a short stroll around the block. If natural light is lacking, try brightening up your home with soft and warm lighting to create a cozy atmosphere.

Create a Quiet Zone

Noise is a considerable generator of anxiety. Creating an area free of noise at home or in the workplace can bring you serenity and focus. This might be a specific room or just a corner where you can go to decompress. Make sure distractions are at a minimum in your quiet zone—turn off the TV, put away your phone, and just relax. Consider using noise-canceling headphones or a white noise machine, especially if you live in a noisy neighborhood.

Add Elements of Nature

No matter how you do it, bringing the outside world inside gives your space a peaceful atmosphere. Plants are especially good at combating anxiety. They improve air quality, introduce a planty ambiance, and add to peaceful enjoyment. Add some indoor plants to your home or office. Grab some succulents, or if you are not the best at tending to plants in general, consider a snake plant. Furthermore, integrating organic elements such as wood, stone, or water features can serve to heighten the calming ambiance.

Personalize Your Space

This environment is constant in the rhythm of our day-to-day lives, and a few small things you can do to promote joy and comfort include surrounding yourself with objects that evoke love and joy. Use your tools daily, such as pencils, pens, or even play some piano music, or just sit outside (think of how beautiful raindrops sound!). Fill your space with what you love, be it photos of loved ones, artwork, or special mementos. Such personal touches can help in keeping the positivity of a place alive and well, providing that feeling of safety and comfort.

Practice Scent Therapy

Using smells to combat anxiety is another powerful tool. Some popular scents that have stress-relieving effects are lavender, chamomile, and sandalwood. You can use these scents through essential oils, candles, or diffusers. Try out different fragrances to see what fits your room the best and use them throughout your space.

- **Other simple daily routines to combat overthinking and anxiety**

Schedule Breaks to Recharge

It's easy to get caught up in the day's tasks and forget to take breaks, but regular pauses are crucial for maintaining mental clarity. Short breaks give your mind a chance to reset, reducing the buildup of stress and preventing burnout.

Tip: Follow the Pomodoro Technique: work for 25 minutes, then take a 5-minute break. After four cycles, take a longer break of 15-30 minutes. Use this time to stretch, take a walk, or simply relax.

Limit Information Overload

In today's digital world, it's easy to become overwhelmed by the constant stream of information. This can contribute to overthinking. Make a conscious effort to limit your exposure to news, social media, and other sources of information, especially during times when you're prone to overthinking. Set specific times during the day to check your phone or watch the news, and stick to those times. This practice helps create mental space and reduces the likelihood of getting caught up in a cycle of overthinking and anxiety.

CHAPTER 5

49

A PERSONALIZED ANTI-ANXIETY PLAN

The purpose here is to create simple and effective ways to help you regain control over your emotions and reduce stress. We all live differently. But you'll definitely find what works for you in this chapter.

- **Developing EQ to better manage stress and anxiety**

First of all, emotional intelligence (EQ) means that you understand your own emotions — and how to manage them along with the emotions of others. Emotional Intelligence: Master your feelings, and you will be able to manage even the most challenging situation cool as a cucumber.

Accept your Feelings and figure out why.

The very first stage of Emotional Intelligence is to know what you are feeling. It is to know how you feel in different situations. When you feel overwhelmed or anxious, pause and name the emotion that is happening. What is frustrating, frightening, or overwhelming you? So naming your emotions helps you identify what is triggering them, and identifying how they are impacting you.

Once you know what your emotions are, the next step is to process them. That likely includes already-mentioned triggers from Chapter 3. What events, people, or thoughts trigger those feelings consistently? Knowing the root behind why you feel a certain way might help to guide what you do about those feelings.

Practice Self-Regulation.

Self-regulation also helps you take a step back when feeling stressed or anxious, in order to avoid impulsive reactions. It allows us the opportunity to make a conscious effort towards our response instead of basing it on emotions running high. Simple techniques like counting to ten allow you the opportunity to chill out and consider a thought through more carefully before responding.

Improve Your Empathy.

Empathy is a key component of emotional intelligence, as it enables you to relate with others and meet their emotions too. Having empathy to a higher degree does also help manage your own stress and anxiety, as perception of different angles enables less isolation.

Build Strong Relationships.

Social relationships also play a significant role in our ability to cope with stress and anxiety. High emotional intelligence people make better friends and co-workers because they are more understanding of how others feel. Having these relationships in place can give you a cushion to fall back on when life gets tough. Every so often, spend some time connecting with friends or family. Open up, be vulnerable and transparent with your feelings, and offer support when someone crosses your path who needs a friend.

Stay Positive.

A daily gratitude practice is a practical way to keep you away from overthinking and make you focus on the brighter side of your life. Write three things you are grateful for each day. These may be as small and simple as a well-timed cup of coffee or massive, life-changing things like that one friend you have. It helps to change your mindset and make you more likely not to wallow in negativity or nervousness by simply ignoring gratitude. With regular practice, it will improve your overall mindset and naturally decrease the amount of overthinking.

- **Self-Compassion (Learning to be kinder to yourself and reducing negative self-talk.)**

Self-compassion is treating yourself as you would a friend (i.e., with kindness and understanding). Most of us are our worst enemies, and when we have a habit of generating negative self-talk, it affects our mental state. By being kinder to yourself, you can diminish that negative self-talk and ultimately increase your happiness quotient along with becoming more resilient.

Recognize and Remedy Negative Self-Talk

Pay attention to the mean things you say about yourself, such as "I am so useless" or "Everything I do is wrong." The first step in changing these thoughts is allowing them to become visible. After you have recognized negative self-talk, the last step is to reframe these thoughts in a more positive and constructive manner. Don't beat yourself up over what you did wrong, just use some balance in looking at the scene. Instead of, "I suck at this," replace it with, "It is okay to fail, and I will only keep learning."

Tip: When you find yourself in self-criticism mode, ask yourself, "Would I say this to a friend?" If it is not, then write the answer to yourself as you would say it to a favorite person in your life.

Self-compassion includes cutting yourself some slack—especially when times get hard. When things do not go as planned, or you feel bad about some mistake, be kind to yourself as you would be in the case of someone else. Even if that means being kind to yourself, letting yourself grieve, or doing one thing each day that gives you comfort and brings you a little bit of happiness.

Let there be Imperfection

No one is perfect, and that's quite alright. Self-compassion is about being human, having faults, and learning from them. Forget about aiming for perfection and simply pursue advancement and evolution.

- **Assessing Your Needs (A step-by-step guide to identifying what works best for you)**

Evaluating your needs is a key step toward creating a life that truly works for you and cultivating a mind free from overthinking and anxiety. It's about understanding what brings you happiness, health, and fulfillment. By taking the time to identify your needs, you can make better decisions, set more effective goals, and create a lifestyle that supports your well-being.

Reflect on Your Current Situation

Start by taking a close look at your current circumstances. Reflect on various areas of your life, such as your health, relationships, work, and personal growth. Consider how satisfied you are in each of these areas. Are there aspects of your life that cause you stress, leave you feeling unfulfilled, or overwhelm you? Understanding your current situation will help you pinpoint areas that need attention.

Next, think about the activities, people, and environments that bring out the best in you. What brings you joy and fulfillment? What makes you feel energized and motivated? Identifying these positive influences will help you understand what you need more of in your life.

Just as it's important to know what makes you feel good, it's equally important to recognize what causes you stress or drains your energy. These stressors could be negative relationships, overwhelming work demands, or environments that don't support your well-being. By identifying these stressors, you can begin to address them and make changes that better support your needs.

Set Clear Priorities and Goals

After reflecting on what's working and what's not, it's time to set clear priorities. What are the most important things in your life right now? What do you want to focus on? Setting priorities helps you allocate your time and energy to the things that matter most to you.

Setting goals is a powerful way to take control of your life, especially when it comes to reducing overthinking and managing anxiety. When you set clear, achievable goals, you give yourself direction and purpose, which can help you focus on what truly matters instead of getting lost in anxious thoughts.

Start by asking yourself, "What exactly do I want to achieve?" Be as detailed as possible. For example, if overthinking keeps you up at night, a specific goal might be to "spend 10 minutes journaling before bed to clear my mind."

Create an Action Plan

Now that you've identified your needs and set priorities, it's time to create an action plan. Think about the steps you can take to meet your needs and improve your well-being. This might involve setting goals, making changes to your daily routine, or seeking support from others. Break your action plan into small, manageable steps and focus on one step at a time.

Reward Yourself

Positive reinforcement is a great way to stay motivated in your journey to overcome anxiety and overthinking. When you stick to your plan for a set period, reward yourself. This doesn't have to be big—it could be something as simple as enjoying your favorite snack, taking a relaxing bath, or watching a movie. Rewards make the process enjoyable and give you something to look forward to.

- **Flexibility (Adjusting as you progress)**

Because this is a tailored approach for anxiety, nothing else matters as much as being able to adapt. Our lives are different.

And well, this thing that we call life presents us with some twists and turns... being too set in our ways can be a recipe for frustration — or burnout.

So this is kind of how flexibility works: it can help you roll with the punches and take things as they come, which will go a long way toward helping you learn from your experiences and avoid spiraling into an anxious, pillow-less nightmare when things don't necessarily go according to plan.

Step 1: Get Used to the Idea of Change

The very first step in becoming more flexible is understanding and embracing the fact that change happens. And you know – no matter how diligent your preparation, something is going to take you by surprise. Rather than considering these setbacks, consider them learning and growth opportunities. If a change is made, stay open-minded and follow channeled changes in your lifestyle to alleviate stress points while keeping inspired.

Check Your Progress As You Go

No number of changes in habits will be much good if you do not check your progress as you go. It lets you know what works, and just as importantly — what does not. You can also tweak your plan to account for any changes in strategy that you pick up, or opportunities, of which there are always millions. Take a day once every week or even month to review your progress. Think about what is working, the challenges you are facing, and whether the current way that things are arranged suits your evolving circumstances.

Be Ready to Change Course

It may be that you find the original plan isn't going as well as expected at some point. It is alright to make a turn and take the other way around. This doesn't mean you're resigned from your goals; it just means that you are approaching them in a smarter way. Don't be scared to try new things. You may try to change an exercise. Allowing the unexpected into your life will take you to better places.

Establish Goals, But Be Flexible

Although you want the goals to be specific (in general, it fights overthinking and anxiety), they can also adapt to how crazy things might get. So, for instance: rather than assigning time-specific targets like "spend thirty minutes at the gym daily," you could aspire to "engage in regular exercise and shoot for 150 minutes per week." That way, you can adjust your routine if you have a full day or if something unexpected comes up.

- **Recognize Setbacks**

Being realistic is one of the key factors of this book. So we must consider the possibility of relapsing into old habits that bring about overthinking and anxiety. While that may happen, it is important to remember that setbacks are a normal part of any journey toward change. What matters most is how you respond to these relapses.

Accept the Relapse without Beating Yourself Up

For starters, when it comes to dealing with relapses, it's important not to be hard on yourself. A spiral of self-criticism can be easy to slip into, but beating yourself up just makes it that much more difficult to get back on the horse. You must accept that you are not perfect and that it is natural to relapse.

Analyze Your Surroundings

At times, the setback may be a product of things outside your control. The more familiar the setting, the less support you have—such as spending time with friends who may not be supportive of your plans or being in places that would trigger past habits—all contribute to a relapse.

Consider Recent Decisions

If you catch yourself making decisions that are not congruent with your new habits or goals, you might be sliding back. While this may seem small—staying up later than you should instead of getting sleep or skipping a meal prep session that was planned—it can lead to huge setbacks down the road.

Find Help

Occasionally, you will need help to balance your needs. Reach out to those who love you and rely on them, or seek professional help if needed. From talking to an advisor, through helpline assistance, or working with a coach/therapist, this can make a big difference in the way you handle your nerves. Identify the people in your life who can be there for you and ask them to help.

Experience

Every relapse is a learning experience. Learn more about yourself and become wiser on your path every time you slip up. Take time to process why it happened and what you can potentially do differently next. If you see these issues as learning experiences, they could effectively speed up your development.

Dealing with relapses has to do with resilience. By recognizing, acknowledging the relapse, understanding what led up to it in the first place (trigger points), reviewing your goals, and most importantly, reaching out for support and learning from this.

Never forget that setbacks are a natural part of progress, the key is not go dwell in them too long, and each time you overcome one, you're building the mental strength to achieve your long-term goals of living life with a mind that's at ease and a glowing confidence.

CONCLUSION

Combatting overthinking and anxiety is a transformative experience that not only brings relief from stress but also opens up a world of opportunities for personal growth.

It is a necessary first step to creating the life you wish for yourself. Once you get over your anxiety, it will help you discover new opportunities in life and give you more confidence in combating challenges.

Now you've made the beautiful progress of reading this book to this point which is a clear sign of your determination.

Remember, growth is not linear. It's a journey of ups and downs, just way more ups than downs. You will have days when you feel every inch on top of the world with your results, and others where everything feels slow or even completely stopped. But remember, all movement, no matter how tiny, is inching closer to where you are trying to head

When the going gets tough, it's easy to lose sight of why you started your journey in the first place. That's why it's so important to stay connected to your "why." Your "why" is the reason behind your goals and the driving force that motivates you to keep going, even when things get difficult.

"Why" Because I want to be a confident person who is at ease with their thoughts.

"Why" Because I want to live healthy (By now, you know how much overthinking amd anxiety affects both the physical and mental health)

"Why" Because I want to excel in my career.

"Why" Because...

Your journey is uniquely yours, and it's one worth pursuing with all your heart. Keep pushing forward, and never lose sight of the incredible person you are becoming. The best is yet to come, and with each step, you are getting closer to the life you've always envisioned. A life with ease, peace, clarity and confidence!

About the Author: Julia L. Ferrati

Julia runs a psychology practice where she deals primarily with singles. During her part-time training, she used the results of this course and her professional practice to write a series of books. She has written several psychological guides on personal development.

Julia lives with her husband and two children in a suburb of Turin, Italy.

Don't miss out!

Visit the website below and you can sign up to receive emails whenever Julia L. Ferrati publishes a new book. There's no charge and no obligation.

https://books2read.com/r/B-A-FVRMB-ATHTE

Connecting independent readers to independent writers.

Did you love *Combatting Overthinking and Anxiety: Living a Happy and Purposeful Life*? Then you should read *Autostima: Scopri le Tecniche per Credere in te Stesso e Raggiungere i tuoi Obiettivi, Aumentare l'Intelligenza Emotiva e Rafforzare la Fiducia in te e Gestire le Emozioni per Migliorare la tua Vita*[1] by Julia L. Ferrati!

[2]

Scopri il segreto per credere in te stesso e aumenta la tua autostima!

Quali tecniche possono aiutarmi ad aumentare la mia autostima? Come posso capire se soffro di bassa o alta autostima? Cosa è necessario fare per ridimensionare la propria

---

1. https://books2read.com/u/38vOnr

2. https://books2read.com/u/38vOnr

L'autostima personale è colei che ci permette di realizzare progetti che a volte ci possono sembrare impossibili, affrontare i problemi e credere di più in noi stessi. Non tutte le persone però nascono con questa particolare dote, ma attraverso tecniche e strategie precise può essere costruita giorno dopo giorno.

Grazie a questo libro scoprirai che cosa è l'autostima e cosa è necessario fare per aumentarla. Conoscerai gli elementi che la compongono e le principali caratteristiche di chi soffre di bassa autostima. Con il test pratico sarai in grado di autovalutarti e in poco tempo passerai all'azione. Le specifiche tecniche e i tanti suggerimenti ti permetteranno di aumentare la tua autostima in tutti i campi della vita, dal rapporto di coppia al mondo del lavoro, in modo da vivere meglio la tua vita!

Ecco che cosa otterrai da questo libro:

Che cosa è l'autostima e i suoi fondamentiGli elementi fondamentali che costituiscono l'autostimaLe caratteristiche di una persona che ha un'alta autostimaCome capire se siamo affetti da bassa o alta autostimaIl test per autovalutarciI vari modi per aumentare la propria autostimaSuggerimenti per aumentare l'autostimaLe azioni da compiere per ridimensionare l'autostimaLa piramide di MaslowLe varie tipologie di distorsioni cognitiveGli step per aumentare l'autostima corporeaDifferenze tra uomini e donneL'autostima nei bambini e nel rapporto di coppiaAutostima nel mondo del lavoro: come aumentarlaLa sindrome dell'impostoreL'autostima al tempo del CovidE molto di più!

Il percorso per aumentare la propria autostima non è semplice, ma neanche impossibile. Con le tecniche giuste è infatti possibile aumentarla in modo da poter ottenere il successo desiderato nella vita di tutti i giorni e sul lavoro!

Also by Julia L. Ferrati

Psicologia

Autostima: Scopri le Tecniche per Credere in te Stesso e Raggiungere i tuoi Obiettivi, Aumentare l'Intelligenza Emotiva e Rafforzare la Fiducia in te e Gestire le Emozioni per Migliorare la tua Vita

Crescita Personale: Scopri il Potere del Pensiero Positivo per Giungere alla Felicità, Credere in te Stesso e Raggiungere i tuoi Obiettivi Personali. La Guida Motivazionale per Arrivare al Successo.

PNL: Scopri la Psicologia Oscura Attraverso le Tecniche Proibite della Manipolazione e Persuasione Mentale, Interpreta il Linguaggio non Verbale Grazie alla Programmazione Neuro Linguistica

Linguaggio del Corpo: Come Analizzare e Interpretare il Linguaggio non Verbale Attraverso gli Atteggiamenti Inconsci, Scopri Come Leggere la Mente e Sviluppare al Meglio la tua Intelligenza Emotiva

Standalone

Combatting Overthinking and Anxiety: Living a Happy and Purposeful Life

About the Author

Julia runs a psychology practice where she deals primarily with singles. During her part-time training, she used the results of this course and her professional practice to write a series of books. She has written several psychological guides on personal development.Julia lives with her husband and two children in a suburb of Turin, Italy.